KEVIN
BARRY

KEVIN BARRY

CARMEL UÍ CHEALLAIGH   12/20

To John,

I hope you enjoy reading
all about this Great Irish
hero!
    Best wishes, Carmel Uí
                     Cheallaigh
                       xxx

MERCIER PRESS

MERCIER PRESS

Cork

www.mercierpress.ie

© Carmel Uí Cheallaigh, 2020

ISBN: 978 1 78117 743 3

A CIP record for this title is available from the British Library.

Printed and bound in the EU.

TO OLIVIA AND DYLAN,
A NEW GENERATION OF READERS.

CONTENTS

PROLOGUE

The Ireland that Kevin Barry was born into at the beginning of the twentieth century was a part of the British Empire; it had been so for hundreds of years.

However, a move to revive Irish culture had begun shortly before Kevin's birth. In 1884, for example, the Gaelic Athletic Association (GAA) had been founded in Co. Tipperary. The aim of the GAA was to preserve and nurture national sports, in particular Gaelic football, hurling and handball. Six years later, in 1892, the Irish National Literary Society was established, encouraging the preservation of Irish customs and literature. The Gaelic League, now Conradh na Gaeilge, followed in 1893, aiming to revive the everyday use of the Gaelic language, as it was felt that speaking and reading in Irish in everyday life was the best way to show that the Irish people were different from the English.

Although the majority of Irish people were Catholics, Protestants were the more powerful, dominant class at this time. But this too was changing. In Dublin businesses, for example, the balance of power was shifting away from Protestants to an expanding group of middle-class Catholics.

The resurgence in all these areas meant that, by 1900, Irish culture was blossoming. In politics, the idea of a free, independent Ireland was also steadily gaining momentum. And during the period of Kevin's short, eventful life, this momentum was to explode into dramatic, tragic action.

1

CHILDHOOD

Kevin Gerard Barry was born at 8 Fleet Street, in the Temple Bar area of Dublin, on 20 January 1902. It was a Monday and, as we will find out, there would be two other significant Mondays in his short life.

Kevin was the fourth of seven children born to Mary and Tom Barry. Most babies were born at home back then and the Barry babies were no exception. Kate Kinsella, who worked as the family's long-time live-in housekeeper, assisted at the birth. It was normal for women to help at home births at the time, if there were no complications. On the other hand, husbands were not allowed in the room under any circumstances, instead forced to pace up and down outside the bedroom door, eagerly awaiting the good news.

Tom Barry was delighted after Kevin's birth. He now had a second son to help him with his farm in Carlow and the successful Dublin dairy business that he ran with his sister, Judith. His sons would carry on the Barry surname for generations to come. Tom must have felt that the future looked very bright for all of them.

In line with the Catholic custom of christening babies shortly after birth – infant mortality was high in those days, with one in five babies dying while still very young – Kevin was baptised the next day in St Andrew's parish church in Westland Row, a short distance from their home. His godparents were his uncle, Jimmy Dowling, and Elizabeth Browne, a neighbour from Carlow. Mr and Mrs Barry were always keen to keep the connection with their native county.

Family records show that the name Kevin

had first entered the family in the early 1800s and had been passed down through the generations. The Barry surname is of Norman origin and Kevin's ancestors came to Ireland in 1170 with the Anglo-Norman invaders. The family originally landed in Cork but, centuries later, fled from that county when the notorious Oliver Cromwell invaded. They kept moving until they finally settled in Tombeagh on the Carlow–Wicklow border.

On Kevin's mother's side, the Dowlings too were strong farmers and lived in Drumguin, across the road from the Barry farm. They were a close-knit family unit, and would continue to be throughout Kevin's life.

***

Kevin had five sisters – Kathleen and Sheila, who were older than him, and Ellen, Mary and Margaret, who were younger. His only brother, Michael, was two years older and his best friend.

All the children attended the Holy Faith Convent in Clarendon Street, which had separate girls', boys' and infant schools. The nuns were strict. Giggling in the yard during breaktime was not encouraged. Clapping their hands loudly, the nuns were known to remark, 'Children, children, Our Lady never laughed.'

Kevin made his First Holy Communion while at the convent and his precious communion medal remains in Tombeagh, in the Barry family home. From a young age, he was proud to serve as an altar boy in St Teresa's Carmelite Church nearby. Prayer was an important part of family life. Tom, Mary, Aunt Judith and Kate would assemble the children at six o'clock each evening as the Angelus bell rang out. After the Angelus, they always recited a decade of the rosary.

Aunt Judith was an astute businesswoman and from Monday to Friday worked tirelessly in the family's dairy business, which at the time was a world where there were very few women.

Still, determined to prove her worth, she dealt with customers and accounts and all the paperwork. On Saturdays, she loved to relax with her nephews and nieces. If the weather was good they made a picnic and walked to St Stephen's Green. Sometimes they took one of the newly electrified trams, wittily nicknamed 'flying snails', to the Phoenix Park, where they would visit the zoo. If the weather was bad she brought them to one of the recently opened Bewley's cafés. There she sampled the fine oriental teas on offer, while the children enjoyed the sticky buns. Judith also often took them to the library. All the children adored books and liked to visit the Kevin Street Public Library, which had opened its doors for the first time in 1904.

One Saturday, when Kevin was about two years old and no longer the baby of the family, Judith decided to take him to the Stanley studio in Westmoreland Street to have his photograph taken. This black-and-white photograph stands on the sideboard in the Barry family home in Tombeagh to this day. It portrays his thoughtful little face as he stares at the camera, wearing the toddler fashion of the day: a dark petticoat covered by a white pinafore, boots and stockings, all topped off with a wide-brimmed straw hat from under which his blond fringe peeps out.

Judith was not the only matronly figure in Kevin's young life. In addition to her other duties, Kate Kinsella watched over the ever-increasing Barry brood. Kate came from a staunch nationalist Ringsend family and, although she could not read or write, she was an excellent storyteller. She recounted tales of the 1798 rebellion, in particular the Battle of Hacketstown in Co. Carlow, a battle that left 300 rebels dead. She told of how the heroic Irish leader of the battle, Michael Dwyer, hid in the Wicklow Mountains for two years afterwards, eluding British soldiers. She taught them rebel songs that she had learned by heart as a child.

Strains of 'The Croppy Boy', 'Boolavogue' and 'Kelly the Boy from Killane' emanated from Fleet Street. During these happy sing-song hours, little did the family suspect that Kevin himself would one day be the subject of probably the most famous of all Irish rebel songs. How chillingly accurate and personal those immortal words from 'Boolavogue' would become: 'For Ireland's freedom we'll fight or die'.

***

One big advantage of being the middle child as he grew up was that Kevin always had someone to play with at home. He spent quiet time indoors with his sisters, making jigsaw puzzles or playing cards and board games. He saved the more boisterous rough-and-tumble games and football for outdoors, and played these with Michael and the other boys who lived on the street.

On Sundays, after Mass, the family often went for a jaunt around the city in their horse and trap. Tom Barry liked to take them out to see the grazing land he rented on the Longmile Road. He kept cows there to supply the dairy. The family also travelled regularly to Tombeagh, which provided a welcome break from the hustle and bustle of city life. They always thought of Carlow as their real home. Fleet Street was more of a business base.

In many ways, Kevin's early life was idyllic. However, these carefree days of childhood came to an abrupt end on 8 February 1908 when Tom Barry died.

Kevin was just six years old.

2

TOMBEAGH, CO. CARLOW

Soon after her husband's death, Mary Barry decided to move back to Tombeagh permanently with four of her children, including Kevin. She left three of the girls with Aunt Judith in Dublin. They continued to study in the convent, while Aunt Judith remained to run the dairy business from Fleet Street.

It must have broken Mary's heart to have to make a hard decision like that. She had to break up her family and deal with the loss of her beloved husband at the same time. Her children were still very young, ranging in age from eleven years down, with only a year or two between each. Afterwards, her second daughter, Sheila, remembered the immediate devastating effect of her father's death on the family: 'Father died in 1908 and things changed. Mother went to Tombeagh and the family was split.' Granny Dowling also moved into the farmhouse in Tombeagh to help Mary and the new housekeeper. Kate Kinsella stayed on in Dublin.

Tombeagh was and still is very much in the heart of the countryside, two miles from Hacketstown and four from Rathvilly in North Carlow. Until 1886, horse-drawn carts brought farmers' produce, such as butter, bacon and poultry, to the Dublin markets. After the train line between Baltinglass and Tullow opened on 1 June 1886, however, life had become easier and more comfortable for trade and travel from Rathvilly train station.

Country life was very different and very quiet compared to life in the big city. There was no electricity and no motor cars. Nonetheless, life on the farm was busy and there were many chores for the two young brothers. Waking early to the sound of cockcrow, they worked alongside the hired farm labourers. Their mother and uncles allocated jobs to all the children. In those days, farming families were self-sufficient. If they needed anything, it was common practice to barter with neighbouring farms.

The Barry farm was primarily a dairy farm, but they also kept chickens, ducks, sheep, a horse and a donkey. They grew potatoes, turnips, carrots, onions, mangolds, wheat and oats. Twice a day, in the morning and evening, the cows were milked. The boys drove the cows into the milking parlour before and after school. After milking, they transferred the milk to the dairy, which was next door to the farmhouse. There it was strained and separated, before being put on milk carts to be taken to Rathvilly train station and, from there, sent to the big dairy in Dublin. Some was churned into butter.

With so many animals, there was always a lot of feeding and cleaning to be done. Collecting eggs from the hen house was an easier job for the younger children. They also wiped the eggs and washed the poultry feeders and waterers. Small hands were good for cleaning the seedling trays and storage bins too.

Each season brought different work. Spring heralded the birth of many new animals: lambs, calves, foals, chickens and ducklings. Planting of crops and cereals began. Summer brought long days in the hayfield. As well as helping with the heavier work of making hay, the boys carried bottles of tea and *caiscín* cake from the kitchen to the men in the fields. Saving hay for winter fodder was essential for the survival of the herd. Short autumn days were spent chopping logs for fires for those long, dark winter evenings when they would listen to tales of long ago. Autumn was also the time for harvesting and gathering of everything sown in the springtime. A draught horse or two pulled the thresher from farm to farm. Neighbours rallied around until every farmer in the community had finished this important work. Grinding mangolds for winter feed for the housed livestock and cleaning out the byre was done by hand.

It was not all hard labour, though. There was plenty of time for fun, games and new hobbies. Seasonal pastimes and activities abounded and intertwined with the farm work. The children foraged for edible fare: they plucked hazelnuts in the wood, picked mushrooms in the sheep-grazed fields, and collected blackberries and gooseberries for making jam and tarts in the farmhouse kitchen. For endless hours, the boys played conkers with freshly gathered horse chestnuts, and chased rabbits, hares and foxes through the hedgerows with friends. They thrived in the freedom of country life and the wide-open spaces. Fishing in the Douglas River at the bottom of the farm was a favourite recreation. This outdoor life suited the growing young boys.

***

Kevin and Michael attended Rathvilly National School. Hitching the donkey to the trap, they travelled to school in style every day.

Edward O'Toole was the principal of this two-teacher boys' school. In 1874, when sixty-six per cent of Catholic teachers were untrained, Edward set out to achieve the highest qualifications in education – and he did. He was a highly respected member of this rural community and was active in all areas of Rathvilly village life. A founding member of County Carlow GAA in Tullow in 1888, for example, he captained the first Rathvilly football team. He was also a member of the Irish Republican Brotherhood (IRB), a secret organisation that aimed to overthrow British rule in Ireland. Combining his parish and professional lives, he instilled in the boys a love of Irish history and a great pride in their area.

Kevin loved the subjects of Rural Science and School Gardening. He revelled in finding and naming rare wild flowers of the district, and was delighted if the teacher could not identify them. Kevin also liked Irish and showed a *grá* for the language early on. The number of people who spoke Irish was diminishing rapidly in Co. Carlow, but the Gaelic League provided courses for teachers to enable them to teach the subject. Special teachers travelled around to many schools teaching the Irish language, Irish dancing and Irish games. Tomás Mac Curtáin, who later became the first republican lord mayor of Cork, was one such teacher.

All of this was going on around Kevin and there is no doubt that Edward O'Toole was a major influence on him during his primary-school education. In his autobiography, *Whist for your life, that's treason*, first published in 1937, O'Toole dedicated a chapter to Kevin. He remembers the Barry brothers joining the school from Dublin and tells us that during lunchtime every day the boys visited the local church. They also loved games, especially Gaelic football.

O'Toole himself is remembered in the village as an excellent but stern teacher. By taking his students on field trips to places of historic importance, he ignited in them a lifelong interest in their local surroundings.

Although Kevin was known to be a quiet and unassuming boy at school, Edward O'Toole's daughter, Nancy, recalls an incident of devilment that Kevin was involved in. She was coming back from the well with two very full buckets of water when she met Kevin and a friend, and, as she explains: 'The pair of them dipped their hands into the water and splashed it all over my long pigtails until my hair was soaked. I did not tell my father how my hair got so wet and I had to make up some story to keep Kevin out of trouble.'

Unfortunately, it was not long before there was more bad news for the Barry family. In April 1912, Aunt Judith died. This was another huge loss for them all, especially her inconsolable nephews and nieces.

3

RETURN TO DUBLIN

Aged thirteen, Kevin returned to Dublin to begin his secondary education. He attended the O'Connell School, run by the Christian Brothers, from April 1915. It was there that he first met and befriended fellow student Frank Flood. However, Kevin only spent a few months in the school, before enrolling in St Mary's College, Rathmines in September 1915. Another famous republican alumnus of St Mary's was Rory O'Connor, who attended the school from 1892 to 1895.

In November 1915 Kevin attended his first republican function. He went to a Manchester Martyrs commemoration concert in the

Mansion House in Dublin with his sister Kathy. The Manchester Martyrs were three Irish republicans (known in their day as Fenians) – William Philip Allen, Michael Larkin and Michael O'Brien – who were hanged in 1867 in Manchester for the murder of a British police officer during an attempt to rescue the Fenian leaders Thomas J. Kelly and Timothy Deasy.

The function had a profound effect on young Kevin. He wanted to join Na Fianna, an Irish nationalist youth organisation that had been founded by Bulmer Hobson and Countess Markievicz in 1909. His family was against it, as he was only thirteen years old, but some within the family believed that he joined anyway. If this was in fact the case, then, in joining, he had taken his first step into the struggle for Irish freedom – a struggle that was about to reach a seismic milestone: the Easter Rising.

The 1916 Rising was an attempt by Irish republicans to overthrow British rule in Ireland and create an independent Irish nation. It was the most significant Irish rebellion since 1798, and was timed for April, during Easter Week, while the British government was busy with the First World War. It began with the reading of the Proclamation – a document declaring Ireland's independence from Britain – by Patrick Pearse on the steps of the GPO on O'Connell Street in Dublin.

After days of intense fighting, with much of Dublin's inner city damaged or destroyed, and having taken heavy losses, the Irish rebels were forced to surrender. Ireland's freedom would have to wait a while longer. Fifteen of the Rising's leaders were executed in May of that year following the failed rebellion.

Kevin probably followed all the developments in the uprising with interest and hope. Afterwards, though, despite his disappointment at the rebellion's failure, he had to turn his attention back to more normal teenage activities, especially school.

***

Belvedere College was Kevin's third and final secondary school. He and twelve other boys moved to there on 1 September 1916 after St Mary's was closed for refurbishment. The fees for Belvedere were four guineas a term. It has always been a stronghold of Jesuit education in Ireland. Like many schools at that time, it was turning out Irish republicans and officers for the British Army in the First World War in equal measure. It was the school of Irish writer James Joyce, while noteworthy republican past pupils included Joseph Mary Plunkett and Cathal Brugha.

While Kevin was in Belvedere, Tom Counihan was there training to be a Jesuit priest. As well as teaching maths and chemistry, he coached the rugby team. Among the teachers, he was undoubtedly Kevin's favourite. They probably grew close when Kevin started playing rugby. He was a substitute on the junior cup team that beat Blackrock College in 1917, which was a miracle by all accounts. An article in the school magazine, *The Belvederian*, noted that, 'K. Barry (forward) always plays a good hard game, a fair tackler, working well in the scrum.'

Rugby wasn't Kevin's only sporting passion, though. In 1918, Belvedere introduced hurling and Kevin played that too.

Aside from his sporting success, Kevin also did well academically. A Mr Fogarty taught French and described him as a 'bright, kind-hearted lad'. It is obvious that Mr Fogarty was not aware of the limerick chanted by the boys (probably including Kevin) behind his back:

Fogarty's nose is long
Fogarty's nose is long
It would be no disgrace
To Fogarty's face
If half of his nose were gone.

For Mr Dempsey, Kevin wrote several English essays. Through these essays we learn a lot about Kevin.

In 'The best way to spend the summer holidays', he tells us it is to go to the seaside because, 'You can get up early in the morning and go for a swim, then get your breakfast and go for a ride on a bicycle, then before dinner you can fish, after dinner you can go out for a sail or a row and then after tea you can go to the pictures.' He goes on to say that Portrush in Co. Antrim is very popular, even though it is 'up in the Orangeman's territory'.

In another essay, entitled 'Prejudice', he writes about religious, personal and racial prejudice, which he believes is worst of all: 'It is divided into two classes, namely that of the white man against the coloured brother, and that of the white man against the fellow white man of a different nation. The two combined form the origins of very many of the world's greatest war and slaughter.'

This is particularly interesting, as it shows a huge awareness, understanding and maturity for someone so young.

'Industrial Unrest' is an essay about businessman William Martin Murphy and the 1913 Dublin Lockout. This was a stand-off where, for five months, workers who were striking for better conditions were locked out by their employers for joining the Irish Transport and General Workers' Union. Coincidentally, Murphy was president of the Belvedere College Union from 1907 to 1919. Undaunted by this fact, Kevin refers to him as a 'grasping capitalist' and to James Larkin, the organiser of the strike, as 'that marvellous leader'. Clearly, even at a young age, Kevin was a person of principle.

Outside of his studies, Kevin made many friends. It was in Belvedere that he first met fellow student Gerry McAleer. Gerry was from Dungannon, Co. Tyrone. The two of them hit it off from the first minute they met and remained best friends for the rest of Kevin's life. Gerry explained that while he was in the pass class, Kevin was in the honours class: 'He was a brighter boy than I was.' According to Gerry, no threat of punishment could ever tempt Kevin to 'let down' a classmate. His friend also tells us that Kevin was 'open-handed, open-hearted and generous to a fault, and first to every manly exercise', but also 'a demon for eating bars of chocolate at school'.

Gerry was the only boy from outside Dublin in the school. He lived with another Tyrone family on the North Circular Road. The McAleers owned a hotel in Dungannon and Kevin stayed there in the summer of 1918. During his stay, local Catholic businessman Sam McManus, one of the few owners of a motor car in the area, drove Kevin and Gerry all over the northern countryside. In a letter home to his sister Kathy, he informed her, 'The longer I stay in the town the better I like it. It is a great place.' In a chatty letter to his mam, he told her about Gerry's elder brother Barney earning five shillings a day to write down the weight of a bale of hay, and sarcastically added, 'very hard work'.

Kevin was involved in other activities outside of his studies, however, including his ever-growing role within the Irish Volunteers.

***

The Irish Volunteers were set up in 1913 as a response to the establishment of the Ulster Volunteers a year earlier. The Ulster Volunteers were formed in opposition to the British government's attempt to establish an Irish parliament under the Home Rule Act. The Irish Volunteers, on the other hand, wanted the introduction of Home Rule at the time.

The Ulster Volunteers were well armed. In stark contrast, the Irish Volunteers had hardly any arms and what they did have were of inferior quality. In fact, the Irish Volunteers regularly drilled with shovels, brushes and hurleys! Many of its members came from groups such as the IRB, the Gaelic League and Sinn Féin.

Ironically, the Irish Volunteer army adopted the same command structure as the British

Army, i.e. companies, battalions, brigades, divisions and, at the top, a general head-quarters. Companies were made up of between sixty and 200 men and were organised at parish level. Companies from the same parish were identified by a letter, for example A Company. Each company had a captain, first lieutenant and second lieutenant. The company captain was called the officer commanding. Battalions consisted of a number of companies from the same geographical area. The number of bri-gades depended on the size of the county, so a small county like Carlow had just one brigade, while a big county like Cork had four.

In October 1917, Kevin joined C Company of the 1st Battalion, Dublin Brigade, and he quickly became an active member. He was fifteen years old. The number of new recruits had surged after the death of Thomas Ashe on 25 September that year. Ashe was a Volunteer from Co. Kerry who had already been to prison for his part in the Easter Rising. Upon his release, he made a series of speeches around Ireland. Within a couple of months he was rearrested for incitement. In August 1917, he was sentenced to two years' imprisonment and sent to Mountjoy Prison. In a bid to have them recognised as political prisoners, he organised a hunger strike among republican inmates there. He died five days later due to injuries sustained while being forcibly fed.

Although Kevin was initially assigned to C Company of the 1st Battalion, he later transferred to the newly formed H Company – which Frank Flood, his old schoolmate from the O'Connell School, also joined. The Volunteers trained at various centres around Dublin. They often went to Finglas on the north side of the city to practice field manoeuvres. It is hard to imagine now, but Finglas was open countryside 100 years ago!

Kevin's first job in the Volunteers was to cycle around the city on Saturday afternoon, usually after he had finished playing a rugby or hurling match, to distribute all the orders for the Sunday morning parades. Often he would not get back home until 11 p.m. No matter how late he went to bed, though, he never missed the 8 a.m. Sunday parade.

By early 1918, random raids for arms by the Volunteers were taking place all around the country. Arrested Volunteers refused to recognise the British courts.

In August that year, *An t-Óglách* magazine succeeded the *Irish Volunteer* as the newsfeed of the Volunteers. Using the tagline 'the official organ of the Irish Volunteer', it provided useful information for the men, including directives from general headquarters and training instructions. Initially published weekly, and then fortnightly, the magazine's office was subjected to regular raids. It is amazing how circulation continued through such turbulent times.

The Volunteers were a military force, but they needed a political party to work alongside in the hope of having an independent Irish government. That is why they keenly supported the Sinn Féin candidates in the December 1918 general election. By distributing leaflets, organising meetings, canvassing voters, and even bringing voters to polling stations, they were instrumental in the success that followed.

Amid all this, Kevin was also managing to stay on top of his schoolwork. In the matriculation examination – the university entrance examination usually held in the final year of secondary school – Kevin obtained honours in English, French, History and Geography, and a pass in Latin. He subsequently won a City of Dublin scholarship to University College Dublin to study medicine. A bright career as a doctor was within his grasp. Regrettably, political events were evolving apace.

4

SOLDIER AND STUDENT

In order to understand the Irish War of Independence, we need to look at the years leading up to 1919.

Following the failure of the 1916 Rising and the execution of its leaders by the British military, the Irish republican party, Sinn Féin, founded by Arthur Griffith in 1905, won a landslide victory in the elections of December 1918. No one was surprised that this revolutionary nationalist party was the overall election winner. After all, the Irish people were sick and tired of their mistreatment by British forces. Voters – including women over thirty, who were eligible to vote for the first time – made their feelings known at the ballot box. Sinn Féin vowed not to send its elected representatives to Westminster, seat of the British parliament. Instead they met in the Mansion House in Dublin on 21 January 1919 to set up an Irish parliament, Dáil Éireann. This first meeting of the Dáil, with Cathal Brugha as acting president, ratified the Proclamation of the Irish Republic that had been issued during the 1916 Rising.

On the same day as the first meeting of Dáil Éireann was taking place, a small band of Volunteers were taking action themselves. They killed two Royal Irish Constabulary (RIC) men who were guarding a load of explosives being taken to a quarry in Soloheadbeg in Co. Tipperary. The first shots had been fired in the War of Independence, marking the start of a two-and-a-half-year-long guerrilla war.

A February 1919 issue of *An t-Óglach* stated: 'The soldiers and police of the invader are liable to be treated exactly as invading enemy soldiers would be treated by the native army of any country.'

On 1 April 1919, the Dáil assembled privately and Éamon de Valera was elected as the first president. The following day Countess Markievicz became the minister for labour. She was the first ever woman elected to parliament and the first female minister in Ireland. It would be sixty years before another woman was appointed to a similar role.

On 10 April, at the second public meeting of the Dáil, de Valera proposed that RIC members be shunned in their communities so that they would not have any information to pass on to the authorities. As a result, all contact with the RIC was forbidden. God help anyone who associated with them because they were punished rigorously. Shops were vandalised for selling goods to them. Undertakers had their hearses burned for burying them. Girl's heads were shaved for courting them! Due to the continuous attacks on rural barracks and the intimidation of policemen's families, resignations from the force increased and the number of new recruits decreased.

In June, de Valera travelled to America to raise money and muster support for the Irish cause. Shortly afterwards, in September, the Dáil was declared illegal by the British administration. Around this time, Michael Collins – affectionately known as the 'Big Fellow' – was juggling three important jobs.

The first was minister for finance, and in this role he launched the daring Dáil Éireann Loan Scheme to raise funds for the new government. Bonds were exchanged for money and the promise of repayment with interest when the British military withdrew from Ireland. Amounts collected at home and in America far surpassed his original targets.

His second job was director of the Irish Republican Army (as the Volunteers were re-named when they took an oath of allegiance to the new Dáil), and he worked hard to turn this into an effective army.

His third role – and this was where Collins had some of his greatest achievements – was as director of intelligence. He developed a sophisticated system that allowed him to gather important information about the enemy through a network of informants and spies working for him. By befriending staff in strategic positions within Dublin Castle – the headquarters for British intelligence in Ireland – the spies were able to pass on details of planned British activities to the IRA, who, in turn, were able to stay ahead of their adversaries. This was a dangerous business, and informers on both sides were shot and their bodies left in public view as a warning to others.

With de Valera away, Collins, a natural-born leader, had a free hand.

Along with the fighting, there was a fake news war. The department of publicity and propaganda produced the weekly *Irish Bulletin* newspaper, starting in November 1919. It showed the IRA in the best possible light while condemning the activities of the British forces. Reports from the Dáil courts and favourable articles from English newspapers featured regularly. Copies were sent to hundreds of international newspaper offices. Accounts of the Irish struggle for freedom spread to every corner of the world. The *Irish Bulletin* proved itself to be a powerful weapon in the fight against the anti-Irish sentiment of English publications like *The Morning Post*. It damaged Britain's portrayal of Irish events and ultimately its reputation abroad.

As all this was going on, Kevin was about to enter university.

***

University College Dublin (UCD) first opened its doors in 1854 as the Catholic University of Ireland, with Father John Henry Newman as its head. It was an alternative to Trinity College

Dublin, which had been set up in 1592 for Protestants.

Kevin entered UCD, renamed in 1882, in the autumn of 1919. There was an unusually high intake of students into medicine that year because it was the first academic year since the end of the First World War. Many young men had died in the war and now the ones who had been too young to enlist were inspired to grab the opportunity of a higher education. The number of women in first-year medicine was unprecedented too. Of the 193 who enrolled, thirty-two were women – a record intake for the time.

Frank Flood was also a student in the 1919–20 academic year at UCD, having won a scholarship to study engineering, as was Gerry McAleer.

Gerry was not active in the republican movement and did not know that his best friend was involved. The two did attend the Literary and Historical Society together, however. This was a debating group for all students, no matter what they were studying. Long established, the society began in 1855. Father Newman, its founder, believed that the true purpose of a university was to provide an opportunity for students from a diverse range of courses to meet, chat and discuss the controversial topics of the day. Although the name suggests that the subjects should be literary or historical, they were usually of political or national significance. Saturday night debates reflected the burning issues of the era, for example 'That constitutional agitation has been a failure in Ireland.'

Male students voiced opinions on many subjects, either as speakers or as members of the audience. While female students attended in droves and often made up half the audience, they rarely spoke.

Once the debate was over, the crowd proceeded to the college bar. There they enjoyed further lively conversation into the small hours.

First World War veterans and staunch republicans mixed freely.

Inside the college walls tolerance of differing viewpoints prevailed, for the most part (although hostility over such issues sometimes spilled into the college, resulting in minor skirmishes and raids). Outside, however, Dublin seethed with tension. Arrests, ambushes, searches and shootings were common. Despite the trouble on the streets, and various curfew hours being imposed, the society kept going.

Away from the society, Kevin was an avid reader. One of his favourite books was *Knocknagow*, a popular novel of the time. Written by the Irish revolutionary Charles Kickham about Irish peasants, and first published in 1879, it remained one of the most read books in Ireland for fifty years after its publication.

Kevin was well-liked throughout the university and made friends easily. A fellow student remembers 'his twinkling eyes and wide infectious grin'.

Overall, as 1919 ended, it was clear that Kevin was enjoying his time in university. It was also clear, however, that 1920 would be an incredibly dangerous year, both for him personally, and for all those who wished to see Ireland free.

5

A NEW AND FINAL YEAR

Dublin remained a lively city in the early months of 1920. Kevin liked to meet friends at the Grafton Picture House for tea at 5 p.m. His sister Kathy remembers that her first act of defiance of British rule was when she didn't stand up for 'God Save the King', the British national anthem, played at the end of a film there.

A selection of light-hearted letters written by Kevin to friends around this time mention going to *céilís* and dancing 'The Siege of Ennis' with girls from Carlow. Commerce dances and enjoying more than a few drinks feature frequently, and he describes one friend as 'rotto' and cursing the effect of alcohol as 'damn booze anyway'. Kevin liked placing bets on horses and relished days out at the Baldoyle Races. In a letter to his friend Bapty Maher, he alludes to being very busy out and about at the 'National Library (ahem)'.

This lively social life enjoyed by UCD students might in some way account for the high failure rate of the first-year medical class of 1919–20. Kevin was amongst this big group. Another reason for his failure, of course, may have been his by now very active secret life in the IRA.

***

In 1920, the scale and intensity of the War of Independence increased.

In February, a curfew was imposed in Dublin between the hours of midnight and 5 a.m. Tanks, lorries and armoured cars combed the streets with searchlights. Frequently, British forces raided houses in the dead of night, charging in with their bayonets ready.

Innocent people were dragged from their beds and any little valuables they had were stolen.

In March, the war took another turn for the worse when Tomás Mac Curtáin, the Sinn Féin lord mayor of Cork, was shot dead in his home in front of his wife and children. Five days later, on 25 March, new recruits for the RIC landed in Ireland, sent by a British administration who would not accept that they were fighting a real war against the Irish. Therefore, they did not send regular troops; they sent the soon-to-be infamous 'Black and Tans'.

The Tans' uniforms were a mixture of army khaki and police dark green. The recruits were mainly ex-army men from the First World War, hired to bolster the RIC's diminishing numbers. They had the power to arrest and imprison anyone at any time. Their mission was to quell the guerrilla warfare in the country by any means necessary.

General Nevil Macready arrived in Dublin Castle in April 1920. His role was commander-in-chief of the British forces in Ireland, counterpart of the dynamic Michael Collins. These forces were particularly concerned by the IRA's small independent units called 'flying columns', formed from men 'on the run'. The units could move quickly over landscapes that were familiar to them. This local knowledge was vital as they were heavily outnumbered. Using the ambush as their main tactic, they often surprised the enemy. Sometimes the ambush resembled a highway robbery, with masked men holding up the RIC and even having shoot-outs at close range. By hijacking post cars and intercepting official British mail, they managed to stay one step ahead of the enemy.

***

On 1 June 1920, after failing some of his exams, Kevin was involved in one of the Volunteer's most effective raids for arms. It was on the King's Inns in Dublin in broad daylight. This was primarily a legal records office for the

British government, but the Volunteers had been told that weapons and ammunition were also stored there. Kevin's bravery in a moment of doubt during the raid – he stepped forward to steady a wavering officer and then led the men in – allowed them to capture a large amount of ammunition, twenty-five rifles, two Lewis guns and other military equipment. No one was hurt in the raid. Kevin and his old friend, Frank Flood, took a souvenir of a bayonet each on this occasion. It was a good haul and a huge morale boost for the men.

After that, Kevin went to Tombeagh for the summer holidays. There he worked alongside his brother, Michael, on the farm, just as they had done as small boys. Saturdays were spent cycling around Arklow, Glendalough and Glenmalure, Co. Wicklow with Michael and other local lads. Distances of fifty miles on the round trip were not unusual for these hardy young chaps. It was customary for them to stop for a few pints in the Woodenbridge Hotel, which has the distinction of being Ireland's oldest hotel.

During this time Kevin was attached to C Company of the 3rd Battalion, Carlow Brigade. Michael Barry was officer commanding in the Tombeagh area. During that summer, C Company – with Kevin playing a part – burned down Hacketstown RIC Barracks on the same night that it was evacuated.

Their next target was Aughavanagh House in a remote part of the Avondale estate in Co. Wicklow. It was rumoured that the British Army were about to occupy it. William Redmond, a member of parliament (MP) for Waterford, lived there.

On a very wet night, fourteen Volunteers, including the Barry brothers, cycled to the house as they had orders to burn it down. However, one of those on the raid, Matt Cullen, recalled that on entering the house they were confronted by Redmond, who denied any knowledge of the British Army's plan and said that as a member of the parliament he would not allow its use as a British barracks. The Volunteers withdrew, telling him he would be shot if British troops ever occupied the house. Less than a year later, British forces did occupy the property, but Redmond was not harmed.

On the cycle home, the weather cleared and the group stopped to rest on a hill in Ballygobbin. Michael later told how Kevin stood up and, looking around him, said, 'God, wouldn't this make you feel the country is worth living for – and dying for.'

***

A pattern of attacks and retaliation by both sides continued throughout the rest of the summer. The Black and Tans committed many atrocities and were despised throughout the country. Burning, ransacking and looting of homes became an everyday occurrence. Intimidation and persecution of women and children were commonplace.

In July, to make matters worse, an elite group called the Auxiliary Division of the RIC (commonly known as the Auxiliaries) began to arrive in Ireland. Made up of ex-army officers, they became arguably even more notorious than the Tans. Both groups adopted increasingly aggressive tactics to defeat the Volunteers. Often they used the excuse of 'trying to escape' as a reason to shoot and kill their hostages; this happened to Dick McKee, Peadar Clancy and Conor Clune in Dublin Castle on the night of Bloody Sunday in November 1920.

On 9 August 1920, the Restoration of Order in Ireland Act became law. It granted the British military comprehensive powers, such as arrest without charge, detention without trial, secret court martials for civilians, and suppression of coroners' inquests. According to the *Irish Independent*, 'It was a measure for the creation of disorder, and anarchy, and the abolition of law.'

Three days after the Act came into force,

Terence MacSwiney, the Sinn Féin lord mayor of Cork, was arrested at a meeting in City Hall. He had succeeded his friend, the murdered Tomás Mac Curtáin, in that job. He immediately went on hunger strike and was transferred to Brixton Prison in London.

The country was in chaos. General Macready himself decried the behaviour of the Tans and Auxiliaries, as he believed a strict code of conduct should be followed by all British personnel. The exasperated secretary of state for war, Winston Churchill, remarked on the situation in Ireland, saying that it was 'monstrous that we have some 200 murders and no one hung'. Prime Minister David Lloyd George agreed. Such cabinet views signalled the course of things to come.

And, on top of all that, Kevin was about to undertake his most dangerous mission yet.

6

AMBUSH AND ARREST

Kevin returned to Dublin in early September 1920, needing to repeat some of his first-year medical exams in UCD. On the advice of his comrades in the IRA, he stayed with his uncle, Pat Dowling, on the South Circular Road, as there was a good chance his own family home would be raided if he stayed there.

The IRA was always looking around for any chance to obtain arms, as it was a small faction faced with the power and might of the British forces. One of its men had noticed an opportunity to seize more arms.

Three times a week, at 11 a.m., there was an army bread collection from Monks' Bakery on Church Street in Dublin city centre. Ten armed soldiers accompanied the lorry picking up the bread. It looked like an easy target. Kevin and some of his fellow Volunteers were determined to make the most of this chance.

The plan was simple: ambush the British Army truck as it collected the bread and grab the soldiers' weapons. Twenty-four men from H Company – including Kevin – were picked to participate in the raid, and two more were chosen to mind the van that would carry off the arms. Even though Kevin had left his own gun, a .45 revolver, in Carlow, he was determined to participate in the raid on the bread lorry. The date chosen for the ambush was 20 September.

The evening before the ambush, Kevin visited Fleet Street for dinner. Mrs Barry later recalled Kevin and Kate Kinsella in the kitchen singing one of Kate's favourite rebel songs written by Peadar Kearney, who also wrote 'Amhrán na Bhfiann', the Irish national anthem.

Neither woman had any idea of what Kevin was planning to do the next day.

***

On the morning of Monday 20 September – the second significant Monday in his life – Kevin went to Mass and received Holy Communion. He was a little late for the meet-up before the ambush, at O'Flanagan's Sinn Féin Club on Bolton Street. His captain, Séamus Kavanagh, was annoyed that he was late and shouted, 'Well this is the only gun I have for you', and handed him a .38 Mauser semi-automatic pistol.

A blackboard was used to outline the details of the ambush, including a map of the area with everyone's position marked. Seán O'Neill, who was second in command, Kevin Barry (section leader) and Bob O'Flanagan, who was the second lieutenant, were to follow the lorry and hold up the soldiers.

Full of excitement and nerves, Kevin was

also conscious of the fact that he was due to take his last exam resit at 2 p.m. that afternoon. He felt confident that he would be finished the ambush in time.

By 10.30 a.m. all the men were in place. Some mingled with people on the streets or read newspapers unnoticed. Others took up inconspicuous positions close by. Two men armed with grenades stood on one of the corners, in case of a surprise attack from the nearby barracks.

The lorry was late. Eventually, at 11.30 a.m., it rumbled up the street. A sergeant went into the bakery, while his men sat on the lorry, waiting. Kevin, Seán and Bob approached, shouting: 'Drop your rifles! Put up your hands!'

All but one soldier dropped their arms. Realising that he wasn't covered – there being only three Volunteers against the five soldiers – that soldier fired at the group of Volunteers. After that it became a free-for-all. Everyone started shooting. Total chaos ensued for what seemed like ages, though in reality the exchange of fire lasted only three minutes.

As a hail of bullets flew around him, Kevin's borrowed gun jammed. We now know that he used non-standard bullets and that semi-automatic weapons were prone to jamming if non-standard ammunition was used. As he tried to free it, his wounded comrades, Seán O'Neill and Bob O'Flanagan, retreated from the scene.

There was a lot of confusion and shouting. As the Volunteers withdrew, 'Bullets were digging up the road,' Bob O'Flanagan recounted later. Kevin slid under the military lorry to take cover and hoped to make a run for it when the lorry moved off.

The sergeant left the bakery to find one of his men dead and two others seriously wounded. A crowd had congregated nearby and some ex-soldiers tended to the wounded. Infantry reinforcements arrived and cordoned off the area. They searched passers-by and raided neighbouring houses. Shopkeepers locked their doors.

The sergeant ordered his men back into the lorry and prepared to drive off. It seemed like Kevin's hiding spot had worked. But suddenly an old woman who owned a shop locally shouted in alarm, 'There's a man under the lorry.'

The soldiers surrounded Kevin and threw him into the back of the lorry with the dead soldier. Eyewitness accounts described the captured man as 'young and good-looking'.

It now seemed certain that Kevin Barry would miss his exam.

***

Surprisingly, there were very few casualties on the Volunteer side. The wounded men attended the Jervis Street Hospital for treatment. Frank Flood guarded the entrance in case the British forces raided.

Meanwhile, Mrs Barry, knowing that Kevin had his final exam resit that day, had sent her youngest daughter, Margaret, to Earlsfort Terrace to watch out for him. Even though it was her birthday, she spent three hours walking around the college, searching for him with no success. She remembered many years later that awful feeling of dread on her way home to her mother, already sensing that something was terribly wrong: 'I think it was one of the most awful things in my life to have to go back and tell her that I hadn't found him.' Soon afterwards, his captain, Séamus Kavanagh, arrived at the Barry household to tell them what had happened.

Kevin was taken to the barracks of the North Dublin Union. He was searched and handcuffed. There he supposedly told Sergeant Banks, 'We were only after the rifles.' A short time later, two officers and three sergeants of the Lancashire Fusiliers entered the room. Then the interrogation began, where he was threatened with a bayonet and had his arm twisted painfully behind his back.

As this was going on, the military were ransacking his Uncle Pat's house. Every item of Kevin's property was taken away.

In the meantime, Mrs Barry and her eldest daughter, Kathy, did the rounds of prisons and their many contacts, keen to get any information on Kevin.

After his interrogation and torture, Kevin was brought to the Bridewell police station for the night. He told his Uncle Pat, who visited him on that first evening, that his arm was excruciatingly painful. From there he was moved to Mountjoy Prison. Prison records describe him as having black hair and blue eyes.

That evening, the board of examiners met in UCD to discuss the resits. Gerry McAleer obtained a pass. Due to the fact that Kevin hadn't completed his resits, he was awarded a fail.

Later that night, the men of H Company returned to the scene of the ambush. They wanted to protect the local people in case of reprisals. Father Albert, the Capuchin priest of 1916 fame (he walked to the firing squad with the rebel leaders), assured them that there would be no reprisals and appealed to them to leave the area.

On 21 September, the day after the ambush, *The Freeman's Journal* – which was the leading nationalist newspaper of the time – led with the headline: 'Fierce Affray in Dublin – Terrifying Scenes in Busy Thoroughfare – Wounded Civilian Captured.'

Things were about to get a lot worse for that 'wounded civilian'.

7

TRIAL

No arms were obtained by the Volunteers in the Monks' Bakery ambush. Five soldiers and three of the raiders were wounded. Three soldiers died. The bodies of Privates Washington, Humphries and Whitehead were transported to England the following week. Four military bands marched in the procession as troops escorted the coffins to Dublin Port. In the weeks after the ambush, Kevin Barry remained in Mountjoy Prison, awaiting trial.

On 20 October, a month after the ambush, Kevin was finally brought in front of a court. He was taken under heavy military escort from Mountjoy to the court martial in Marlborough (now McKee) Barracks. It was a wet and dismal morning. He was twenty-five minutes late because the armoured car he was travelling in broke down and they were forced to wait for a relief car.

Everyone entering the court that morning, including the journalists, were searched. His mother, his uncle Pat Dowling, the family solicitor Seán Ó hUadhaigh, Father Augustine, a republican Capuchin priest, Eileen O'Neill and Gerry McAleer, who were his close friends, and Joe Farrell, a close family friend, were there.

Kevin was charged under the Restoration of Order in Ireland Act with feloniously wounding and killing Private Whitehead. This was the first case in which a person was tried for a capital crime under the new Act. He told the court that as a soldier of the Irish Republic he regarded all of his actions as acts of war. As a republican, he refused to recognise the court and did not put forward a defence.

The crown summoned sixteen witnesses.

Witness after witness gave their version of events of the morning of 20 September. After each testimony Kevin was asked if he wanted to cross-examine the witness, but he declined and eventually snapped: 'Don't bother asking me that question any more, I am not interested in the proceedings.'

Two witnesses testified to having seen the accused fire a pistol into the army lorry just before Private Washington fell dead, shot through the chin. A bullet found in Private Whitehead's body was of the same calibre as the ones in Kevin Barry's pistol, which had been recently fired. However, any of the other raiders could have had a similar gun. The most incriminating evidence was the alleged admission by the accused shortly after the arrest that 'We were only after the rifles.' This clearly placed him with the raiders.

The trial was rigged against Kevin from the start. The jurors were members of the British Army. No independent witnesses were called to give evidence. All the witnesses were members of the British military. None of these witnesses were cross-examined. While forensic examination of bullets didn't conclusively prove that Kevin's gun fired the bullet that killed Private Whitehead, the fact that he was present meant that he was guilty by association and that was enough. A conviction was inevitable. Soon the trial ended and the prisoner was sent back to Mountjoy.

Kevin's comrades had a plan to rescue him during the trial, which involved capturing an armoured car. The car was at a nearby bank collecting wages for military staff, commanded by a one-armed officer. In the end, though, the seizure of the car didn't happen. Some say it failed because the Volunteers didn't want to fire on a handicapped officer.

Back in Mountjoy that evening, Kevin was told of the verdict in his cell. He had been found guilty and sentenced to death by hanging.

8

CALLS FOR A REPRIEVE

In the final days of October, international newspapers were focused on Ireland. People around the world were already enraged by the tragic death of Terence MacSwiney after seventy-four days on hunger strike on 25 October. How could an elected representative die a slow painful death like this at the hands of Britain? The Kevin Barry story also appeared in many English newspapers.

In a 'message to the civilised world', Arthur Griffith declared:

It may be in the power of England to hang an Irish boy of 18 under such circumstances but it is not in her power to prevent the conscience of mankind reprobating with horror such an action.

On 27 October, Kevin was informed that the execution would take place the following Monday, 1 November, at 8 a.m. Still, even at this point, few believed the British authorities would hang him.

In both Ireland and England there were calls for a reprieve. But there was very little time. Kevin's fate aroused much attention, including from Pope Benedict XV, who suffered much anxiety over the callous treatment and death sentence handed down to one of his flock. He spoke with British diplomats in the Vatican. Ernest Aston, who was Kathy Barry's employer and well in with the British authorities, travelled to London to plead with Prime Minister Lloyd George for leniency for Kevin. Many letters were written to newspapers. Edward O'Toole wrote a letter to Joseph Devlin, MP, asking him to do whatever he could to prevent the execution of his former pupil. Archbishop Walsh of Dublin and the city's lord mayor, Larry O'Neill, called to Lord Lieutenant French in the viceregal lodge in the Phoenix Park and asked him to revoke the death sentence. The lord mayor followed up the visit with several phone calls before finally sending a telegram to Lloyd George.

On 28 October, Kevin was informed by his sister Kathy of an order from Dick McKee, a senior member of the republican movement, that he was to make a statement about his treatment and questioning. It was hoped that this would put further pressure on the British government to reverse its decision. After all, time was running out.

Seán Ó hUadhaigh prepared the statement, which Kathy was then to pass to the Sinn Féin director of publicity to send to the English newspapers for publication that weekend. So, on the day after receiving the news of his death sentence, Kevin made the following statement:

I, Kevin Barry, of 58 South Circular Road in the County of the City of Dublin, Medical Student, aged 18 years and upwards, solemnly and sincerely declare as follows:

On the 20th day of September, 1920, I was arrested in Upper Church Street, in the City of Dublin, by a sergeant of the 2nd Duke of Wellington's Regiment, and was brought under escort to the North Dublin Union, now occupied by the military. I was brought into the guardroom and searched. I was then removed to the defaulters' room by an escort with a sergeant-major. The latter and the escort belong to the 1st Lancashire Fusiliers. I was then handcuffed.

About a quarter of an hour after I was placed in the defaulters' room two commissioned officers came in. They both belonged to the 1st Lancashire Fusiliers. They were accompanied by three sergeants of the same unit. A military policeman who had been in the room since I entered it remained. One of the officers asked my name which I gave. He then asked the names of my companions in the raid or attack. I refused to give them. He tried to persuade me to give the names, and I persisted in refusing. He then sent the sergeant out of the room for a bayonet. When it was brought in the sergeant was ordered by the same officer to point the bayonet at my stomach. The same questions as to the names and addresses of my companions was repeated, with the same result. The sergeant was then ordered to turn my face to the wall and point the bayonet to my back. I was so turned. The sergeant then said he would run the bayonet into me if I did not tell. The bayonet was then removed and I was turned round again.

The same officer then said to me that if I persisted in my attitude he would turn me out to the men in the barrack square, and he supposed I knew what that means with the men in their present temper. I said nothing. He ordered the sergeants to put me face down on the floor and twist my arm. I was pushed down on the floor after my handcuffs were removed by the sergeant who went for the bayonet. When I lay on the floor, one of the sergeants knelt on the small of my back, the other two placed one foot each on my back and left shoulder, and the man who knelt on me twisted my right arm, holding it by the wrist with one hand, while he held my hair with the other to pull back my head. The arm was twisted from the elbow joint. This continued, to the best of my judgement, for five minutes. It was very painful. The first officer was standing near my feet, and the officer who accompanied him was still present.

During the twisting of my arm, the first officer continued to question me as to the name and addresses of my companions, and also asked me the name of my company commander and any other officer I knew.

As I still persisted in refusing to answer these questions I was allowed to get up and was again handcuffed. A civilian came in and repeated the questions, with the same result. He informed me that if I gave all the information I knew I could get off. I was then left in the company of the military policemen; the two officers, the three sergeants and the civilian leaving together.

I could certainly identify the officer who directed the proceedings and put the questions. I am not sure of the others, except the sergeant with the bayonet. My arm was medically treated by an officer of the Royal Army Corps, attached to the North Dublin Union, the following morning and by the prison hospital orderly afterwards for four or five days.

I was visited by the court-martial officer last night and he read for me a confirmation of sentence of death by hanging, to be executed on Monday next, and I make this solemn declaration conscientiously believing same to be true and by virtue of the Statutory Declarations Act, 1835.

Kevin Gerard Barry

Declared and subscribed before me at Mountjoy

Prison, in the County of the City of Dublin, the 28th day of October, 1920.

Myles Keogh

A Justice of the Peace for the said County.

As his statement explains, he was not medically treated until the morning after his 'interrogation'. When his mother visited him eleven days after his arrest, his arm was still in a sling. This appalling treatment was later referred to as 'The Torture of Kevin Barry'.

Unfortunately, Kevin's statement was not published in time. However, it is likely that, even if it had been published straight away, nothing would have changed. General Macready opposed a reprieve on all grounds. The British authorities did not think the arguments about Barry's age and the negative effect his death would have on Irish public opinion were strong enough grounds for a reprieve. They were more worried about the effect on morale in the British forces if he wasn't punished.

Despite the widespread outcry, they were determined to hang Kevin Barry.

9

CONDEMNED CELL

Hundreds of thousands of prisoners have passed through the doors of the historic Mountjoy Prison in its 170-year history. They include the historical figures of Éamon de Valera and Countess Markievicz, who were incarcerated there following the 1916 Rising. Kevin had already spent exactly one calendar month in Mountjoy before he was moved to the condemned cell the day after his trial.

Up to that point all his meals had been brought into him by dear, kind Kate Kinsella. He always preferred Kate's cooking. The day after his trial, however, she was not allowed in. That was when she knew he must have been found guilty. Devastated, she returned to Fleet Street and stayed in her room, where she cried for hours. The thought of him dying was unbearable. She had been at his birth and did not want to witness his death too.

Built in 1850, the cells were meant for one person only. Most measured 3.43 x 2.06 metres, but the condemned cell was much bigger. In fact, it was about three times the size, with nearly a third of it taken up by the toilet. It was also the only cell with a fireplace. The cell was at the end of D Wing, mere yards from the 'hang house' where all the executions took place by hanging. Kevin's breakfast was bread and butter, with bacon and tea, while dinner was beef, or fish on Fridays, with potatoes, and supper was bread and milk.

***

In the lead-up to his planned execution, Kevin's birth certificate arrived at the prison. The authorities needed it to confirm that he was not underage, as the legal age for executions was eighteen. Unable to sign her name, Kate Kinsella had marked an X as a witness to his birth.

During his final days in Mountjoy, Kevin exercised in the small yard to the back of his cell. He walked around the yard accompanied by two wardens. Armed prison guards kept a close eye on him from several vantage points. Kevin was popular with the prison guards after giving one of them a tip for a winning horse, Busy Bee, running on 22 September.

As he walked the yard, he had a good view of the execution chamber. He could sometimes hear someone working inside. Essential repairs were needed, it turned out, as the last time someone had been hanged there was nearly twenty years earlier.

Kevin was a soldier and did not want to be executed like an ordinary criminal. Firing squad was the most common method of execution then for soldiers of the Irish Republic. He told his sister Kathy: 'I'd rather be shot.'

He had many visitors on those final days. On 28 October, nuns from the Sisters of Charity in Gardiner Street visited him. As religion had always been important to him, he was glad to see them. He read many holy books during those final, sombre days. On hearing that the nuns set aside one day every month to prepare for death, he commented, 'You must be very good.'

That same day Gerry McAleer also visited. Wondering about who signed the death sentence, he asked, 'Was it Macready?'

'For all I know or care it might have been Charlie Chaplin,' Kevin replied.

Kevin tried to keep his friend upbeat. 'I'd like to leave you something,' he said. 'I would leave you my shoes only I couldn't very well walk barefoot to the scaffold.'

The next day, Kevin wrote to Gerry. 'I was glad to see you yesterday looking so fit and well,' he began. He ended the letter by sending his

best wishes to the second-year medical students
and asking them to 'say a prayer for me when
I go over the top on Monday'. The letter was
written with a purple pencil. All letters had to
be read and checked by the prison governor in
case there was anything problematic in them.

Kevin requested a visit from Father Augustine, who visited twice, on 29 and 30 October.
He blessed Kevin and they prayed together and
spoke about St Francis of Assisi. Father Augustine gave Kevin a scapular and cross and
welcomed him into the Franciscan order for
lay people. Kevin said that he was 'praying for
courage' and the priest, aware of the kind of
death awaiting him, said, 'And you'll have it,
Kevin. Before they touch you, St Francis will
have hold of you by his *cord,* and will welcome
you to Heaven.'

Between visits, Kevin signed his name
and new address on the title page of his copy
of *Knocknagow*. He labelled himself as 'A
dangerous criminal' and 'A decided menace

to the British Empire' on the opposite page. Scribbling his crimes as 'putting pepper in the cat's milk, stealing a penny from a blind man and smiling derisively at a policeman', he whiled away the long hours, never losing his sense of fun.

***

As the days and hours counted down, further plans were made by the Volunteers to rescue Kevin. The second rescue plan was to break him out while his sisters were visiting him on the Saturday afternoon before the execution. It was timed for shortly before the changing of the guard at 4 p.m. However, the girls' visit was delayed due to the arrival of a tall priest, probably Father Brennan of Hacketstown, to visit Kevin, meaning the rescue attempt couldn't go ahead.

Another plan was for the Volunteers to disguise themselves as British reinforcements who were due to arrive at the jail. This plan too had to be abandoned when it was discovered that the real reinforcements had already arrived at Mountjoy.

The final plan was set for the Sunday night before the execution and involved using a home-made bomb to blow a hole in the prison wall. It was called off, however, as the Volunteers realised that Kevin would be shot immediately if there was any trouble, and it was also felt that this plan could cause the death of civilians outside the prison.

Seán O'Neill, who had been part of the Monks' Bakery ambush, was due to act as a sniper in the first rescue attempt and was ready to take out the guards at the main gate as part of this final plan.

Ultimately all these plans were considered too risky. Kevin was heavily guarded at the court and at the jail. Rescuing him was never a realistic option.

But Kevin did not want a reprieve or to be rescued. He had stated emphatically to his sister Kathy: 'Mind, there's to be no appeal.' The Barry family were determined to respect Kevin's wishes.

***

On Sunday 31 October, Terence MacSwiney was buried in Cork. As one martyr was being buried, the gallows were being prepared for another. In America, *The Chicago Tribune* implored its readers to 'Pray for the condemned Boy'. In Dublin, Tom Counihan received a message to visit his former student. Afterwards he described Kevin as 'the calmest man in the prison'.

The place was swarming with Black and Tans, which was unusual for Dublin, as they were mainly concentrated in the areas outside the capital. This heightened security reminds us of how seriously the British took the threat of someone trying to rescue Kevin, or perhaps they were concerned about the possibility of riots after Kevin was hanged.

At around 4.30 p.m., his mother, sister Kathy and brother Michael arrived at the prison. How difficult a visit it must have been for all of them, realising they would never chat with him again in this life. As they were leaving, they turned around one last time and he was standing at the salute. Wearing his trench coat with the collar turned up, it was the nearest thing he had to a soldier's uniform.

That walk away from her youngest son was, without doubt, the most painful walk Mrs Barry ever experienced. Memories of him as a baby, cradling him in her arms; as a toddler, scolding him to keep him safe; as a young boy, running and playing with his siblings; and of the more worrying teenage years, all flooded back. Remembering Halloween night over the years, the children bobbing for apples in the kitchen, she could still hear their laughter as if it were yesterday. Halloween would be a night of sorrow from then on, as she faced every parent's worst nightmare in the loss of her son.

In the natural order of things, a parent goes first. In addition, he had such a bright future ahead of him.

Determined not to let him down, she held her head high as she passed by the British forces. Her pain was unbearable, but she refused to break down in front of them. In the corridor she met Canon Waters, one of the prison chaplains, for the first time. He told her that he was not sure if Kevin knew that he was about to die as he was so cheerful. She told him, 'Canon Waters, can't you actually understand that my son is proud to die for the Republic?'

Outside, hundreds of UCD students recited the rosary. Father Albert asked for a last-minute visit with Kevin, which was granted. The two men spoke in Irish. Albert told him about the students praying outside and he was visibly affected by this. His parting message to the priest for those outside was: 'Hold on. Stick to the Republic.'

Later that Sunday night, Michael Collins

entered Vaughan's Hotel in Parnell Square. Kevin's impending death weighed heavily on his mind. He did not talk to anyone. Every now and then he muttered the words: 'Poor Kevin Barry.' Collins knew that many Fenians had gone to their death unsupported by words from their leaders. But he felt powerless at the thought of young Kevin Barry facing his fate alone.

Not far away, John Ellis, the English hangman, had arrived in Mountjoy. He was busy checking the new ropes.

10

'ANOTHER MARTYR FOR OLD IRELAND'

Kevin slept soundly until 6 a.m. He awoke to another significant Monday: 1 November, his final one. It was a cold morning and still dark when a large crowd of people started to gather outside the prison. Gas lights flickered on the streets. An armoured car patrolled the area. A lorry-load of heavily armed soldiers was on standby in case of trouble. A group of Cumann na mBan marched across the city from St Stephen's Green.

At 7 a.m., the two prison chaplains arrived from Clonliffe College. Canon Waters and

Father MacMahon were admitted to the prison through a small side door. Coincidentally, Father MacMahon was a former lay member of staff at St Mary's College, Rathmines, the school where Kevin was a student from 1915 to 1916. Kevin greeted them cheerily and calmly. First Canon Waters heard his confession. Then the canon said Mass at the little altar prepared earlier by Kevin and a prison warder. The only light in the cell came from the altar candles. Kevin and the warder both received Holy Communion.

Around the same time, the Barry family attended Mass in Clarendon Street. In Tombeagh, Kevin's impending death was felt especially severely. Neighbours and friends gathered at the Barry farm and prayed. All around the prison, the republican inmates recited the rosary from 7.15 a.m.

Before leaving the condemned cell, Kevin signed his prayer book 'K G Barry 1 November 1920'. This prayer book is still in Tombeagh today, in the Barry family home.

In Ireland, it was the tradition to have two priests present at an execution. Kevin walked to his death in the hang house flanked by the two chaplains. All the time they prayed together. Inside the chamber was neat. The rope hung from a chain attached to a beam in the ceiling. The two hinged trapdoors in the upper room were now level with the floor. The hangman was waiting.

It was nearly 8 a.m. and everything was ready for the planned execution. Kevin's arms were pinned back with leather straps. He told the hangman and his assistant that he did not want this because he was a soldier and not afraid to die. Nonetheless they strapped his legs tightly together. The hangman pulled a white linen cap down over his face. Then he adjusted the noose around Kevin's neck, released the safety pin and pulled the lever.

It was all over in less than ten seconds. Father MacMahon anointed the body shortly afterwards. As the death bell rang out over the city, the crowds fell still outside.

The clank of the prison gate opening interrupted the silence. It was Canon Waters leaving the prison. Surrounding him, the waiting crowds asked questions as to how Kevin had died. 'Bravely,' he answered, tears welling up in his eyes. Then a warder came out and stuck the typewritten death notice on the prison wall. It read: 'The sentence of the law passed on Kevin Barry, found guilty of murder, was carried into execution at 8 o'clock this morning.'

Before dispersing, the crowd recited the sorrowful mysteries of the rosary in Irish. After one hour the body was cut down by the prison warders. The republican prisoners sang 'Faith of our Fathers', 'Wrap the Green Flag Round Me' and 'God Save Ireland' in honour of their brave comrade, before attending Mass at 10 a.m. No inquest was held. This was in accordance with the new rules laid down by the Restoration of Order in Ireland Act.

Kevin's body was put into a prison-made, plain deal coffin and the chaplains buried him around 1.30 p.m. Only prison officials were allowed to attend. He was buried in a quiet laurel plot near the women's prison, in unmarked, unhallowed ground. He was the first political prisoner executed since the 1916 leaders were shot in Kilmainham Gaol.

All around the country, Masses were said in Kevin's name. News travelled fast. Churches were full as it was a holy day of obligation. (1 November, the feast of All Saints' Day, is an important feast day in the Catholic Church.) The British government had not taken into account the significance of the date for the people of Ireland. By selecting 1 November to execute Kevin, they immediately made a martyr of him. This date added to the perception of him as saint-like. Neither did they understand the devout and emotional nature of the Irish. This would prove their undoing.

11

AFTERMATH

In the hours following Kevin's death, the whole country mourned. A dark cloud of frustration and despair hung over the country. A telegram was sent to the extended family in Carlow, informing them of Kevin's execution. By 11 a.m. the news had reached Rathvilly. Second Mass was said for the repose of the soul of the recently departed son of that parish, the parish of his ancestors. Sympathy was expressed to the Barry family. Callers to Fleet Street offered their condolences.

Led by sixteen-year-old Seán MacBride, a group of students raised the Irish tricolour at half-mast in UCD. The Literary and

Historical Society members were numbed with the shock of his loss. One hundred and fifty British soldiers arrived in armoured cars and raided UCD the day after the execution. Second-year medical students were identified and searched in case they were connected to Kevin's activities. As the hunt for arms and incriminating documents in the dining hall got underway, surprised student Volunteers handed over weapons to guileful waitresses to hide. Fortunately, most were in Cumann na mBan or supported the republican cause.

In Hacketstown, the tricolour flew for two days until the military came and pulled it down.

According to the *Irish Independent* of Thursday 4 November, most of the baby boys born on Tuesday and Wednesday that week were named Kevin. *Le Matin*, the Parisian newspaper, criticised the 'relentless repression' by the British authorities.

Over the following days, Mrs Barry received a letter from Canon Waters containing Kevin's prayer book and a small Sacred Heart card with the inscription 'To Mother from Kev, on the eve of his death.'

The public outcry increased when Kevin's statement was finally released. Ordinary decent members of the British public did not like being represented in this way. Newspapers at home and abroad used it as a way to bolster support for the Irish cause.

There is no doubt that the mistreatment of Kevin Barry proved significant in turning Irish public opinion against the British forces, and was ultimately a factor in leading Ireland to gain its independence a few short years later. In a powerful letter to the *Westminster Gazette*, a keen supporter of the Irish republican cause, Erskine Childers, wrote:

> To hang him for murder is an insulting outrage, and it is more, it is an abuse of power, an unworthy act of vengeance, contrasting ill with the forbearance and humanity invariably shown

by the Irish Volunteers towards the prisoners captured by them.

The IRA routinely released British forces they captured once their arms were taken from them.

Kevin's death became an international media event. Newspapers were the main source of information at the time, and since the beginning of the War of Independence, around the world large sections of them were given over to reporting on the war and the reign of terror inflicted on the Irish. Most were sympathetic to the plight of the Irish people, particularly in America where there had been a huge influx of Irish immigrants after the Great Famine of 1845–1849. From the Atlantic to the Pacific coasts, the American newspapers had their say. *The Boston Globe*, in late December 1920, published an article about 300 medical students in Tufts College denouncing the torture and execution of their fellow medical student in Ireland. They passed a resolution condemning the British government for its 'uncivilized actions'. *The New York Tribune* and *Los Angeles Daily News* carried articles and poems about Kevin.

British newspapers were more divided in their accounts. *The Manchester Guardian* criticised the British government in a bid to counteract the anti-Irish sentiment spewed out by *The Morning Post*. *The Daily Mail* stressed the fact that the dead soldiers were mere youths too.

The Freeman's Journal, founded in 1763, was the leading Irish newspaper in the nineteenth and early twentieth centuries. As many people could not read or write, it was read to them by priests or teachers at gatherings in the community. On 2 November, coverage of Kevin's execution dominated the paper. The front page led with the headline 'School-Boy who died', showing a photograph of Kevin underneath. A photograph of the huge crowd outside the prison also featured.

***

The death of Kevin Barry was a moral turning point in the War of Independence. It was a step too far. Kevin's death contributed to the eventual establishment of the Free State of twenty-six counties, as it brought people to the negotiating table. However, Kevin was not the only Barry to join the fight for Irish freedom; other family members also took part in the struggle after Kevin's martyrdom.

Michael Barry was arrested on 31 December 1920 in a car full of hand grenades and sent to Lincoln Prison in England. There he remained for fourteen months. In the meantime, neighbours and friends rallied around to help with the farm. Gerry McAleer was arrested for what he describes as 'his part in making the hay'. He was brought to Carlow Barracks and then on to the Curragh internment camp, where he was held for three weeks.

Kathy Barry joined Cumann na mBan in late 1920 and continued to strive for Irish independence. She worked closely with Collins and de Valera. In 1922 she travelled to America with Countess Markievicz on a two-month tour to speak for the republican cause. It was a gruelling tour across the country. One of the things the two women always did was inspect the local jail wherever they were, and in particular the condemned cell. Two years later, Kathy married Jim Moloney, a republican who had fought in the War of Independence. Shortly afterwards she embarked on a Sinn Féin fundraising and publicity tour of Australia.

Sheila Barry was active in a Carlow branch of Cumann na mBan during the War of Independence. In 1924, she married Kevin's old friend Bapty Maher and moved to Athy, County Kildare.

Ellen Barry, aged eighteen, was one of 400 women imprisoned during the Irish Civil War in 1922 and ended up in the North Dublin Union where, two years earlier, her brother had been 'interrogated' by the British. It had been converted into a jail as Kilmainham Gaol was full. In sympathy with the Kilmainham prisoners, the women went on hunger strike.

The Barrys were, without doubt, an heroic family.

***

The Anglo-Irish Treaty was signed on 21 December 1921, ending the War of Independence. It was ratified by the Dáil on 7 January 1922 and 400 political prisoners sentenced in Ireland before the Truce were released under an amnesty. Unfortunately, this was just a temporary solution to Ireland's problems. Éamon de Valera rejected the Treaty, which had been signed by Michael Collins, and they became leaders of opposing factions in the bitter Irish Civil War that followed, where former comrades were cast against each other and families and parishes were split.

During a discussion with Michael Collins about the Anglo-Irish Treaty in early 1922, Kathy Barry retold a conversation she had

had with Kevin in which he said, 'When this damned Dáil takes Dominion Home Rule, they needn't expect us to back them up.'

On this evidence, it is clear that he would have been on the anti-Treaty side had he lived. As well as that, though, it's also clear that he would have hated to see comrade fighting comrade – even if his great composure and courage as he faced death became an inspiration for those who continued to fight and who went on to change the course of Irish history forever. This was some little consolation for the heartbroken Mrs Barry, who was always proud of her son, though devastated by his loss, right up to her death in 1953.

12

GLASNEVIN CEMETERY

Kevin Barry was the first and youngest of the ten men hanged during the War of Independence. His old friend and fellow student Frank Flood would be buried close by him just four months later. Both men were part of the group now known as 'The Forgotten Ten'. Flood, Patrick Moran, Thomas Whelan, Thomas Bryan, Patrick Doyle and Bernard Ryan were all hanged on 14 March 1921; Thomas Traynor on 25 April 1921; and Edmund Foley and Patrick Maher on 7 June 1921. All ten were hanged because they were soldiers of the Irish Republic fighting before the Truce of July 1921. A simple cross marked their graves in Mountjoy Prison until 1961, when President Éamon de Valera unveiled a set of new gravestones.

In 1923, relatives of 'The Forgotten Ten' began a campaign to have the remains of their loved ones reinterred. All they wanted was a proper funeral service and burial in consecrated ground for their family members. Requests to release the bodies shortly after their executions had been rejected by the new Irish authorities. A few years later the National Graves Association (NGA) added its voice to the movement. The NGA had been established in 1867 and pledged to restore and maintain patriot graves and to commemorate those who died in the name of Irish freedom. In 1934, the NGA marked the burial plot of the men within the prison walls and maintained it down through the years. In 1996 a Celtic cross was erected in Glasnevin Cemetery for 'The Forgotten Ten'.

Then, on 14 October 2001, Kevin was finally freed from within the prison walls, along with his nine comrades. Eyewitness reports from the exhumation in Mountjoy stated that Kevin's waistcoat and a tiepin, cufflinks and armband all of silver were dug up with his remains. All the skeletal remains were found as they had been buried, lying on their backs with arms folded in a reverent manner.

It was to Glasnevin cemetery that Kevin was eventually removed. It was the preferred burial place as it had a reputation of being a republican cemetery. Nine of 'The Forgotten Ten' were moved here, while Patrick Maher's remains were brought to his home area of Ballylanders, Co. Limerick.

The day of their burial in Glasnevin began with a buffet breakfast in Dublin Castle for 600 relatives. Some had travelled long distances from America and even Saudia Arabia to be there. Then they were transported by bus to Mountjoy. There, ten coffins stood over the exact spot of the former burial plots, Irish tricolour flags draped over each one. Relatives transferred the coffins on their shoulders to the waiting hearses. The original prison bell tolled and staff lined the route to the front gate. Soft October rain fell from the sky as the cortege left the prison.

Once outside, the Defence Forces moved forward and flanked the long procession of hearses. The families walked behind. It was a great consolation for them, even though it had taken far too long, that the Irish State was now formally recognising that the ten men were soldiers who had fought and died for Ireland. Thousands of well-wishers lined the route, applauding and waving Irish flags. Thousands more watched the funeral procession on television as it passed through Dublin city centre. A lone piper played a mournful tune as the cortege passed the GPO, the headquarters of the 1916 Rising.

Priests from the Capuchin Order con-celebrated the requiem mass with Cardinal Cathal Daly at St Mary's Pro Cathedral. The cathedral choir sang 'Ag Críost an Síol' as the coffins were carried to the altar. Michael Barry, Kevin's grandnephew, carried a gift to the altar as part of the offertory procession. Then it was on to Glasnevin Cemetery for the final part of their journey.

Wreaths were laid by the families and then An Taoiseach Bertie Ahern gave the graveside oration in Irish and English. A volley of shots rang out over the graves as the men were buried with full military honours. The day's ceremonies ended with the playing of 'The Last Post'. Kevin Barry and Frank Flood were side by side once more.

Kathy Barry Moloney, Kevin's eldest sister and great friend, lies near to Kevin now. She died in 1969 and is buried with her husband James and two of their children in the cemetery.

Kate Kinsella is also nearby. She was eighty-four when she died in 1937. Loyal, devoted, faithful servant Kate joined Ellen Barry, an unmarried dairywoman and grandaunt of Kevin, who died in 1883. This shows us the high esteem in which Kate was held by the family. She was much more than an employee. Tom Barry erected the headstone. Many others who were part of Kevin's life are buried there too, including Seán (John) O'Neill from H Company, who was with Kevin on 20 September, the day of the bakery raid, and who was so keen to participate in two rescue attempts. He died on 23 May 1965.

Another character from that fateful day who now resides in Glasnevin is Catherine Garrett – the old shopkeeper who alerted the soldiers to Kevin under the lorry. She died on 29 August 1923.

***

Many of the other republicans mentioned in this book are buried in the Republican Plot in Glasnevin Cemetery. These include:

Thomas Ashe: His body lay in state for two days in City Hall where an estimated 30,000 mourners filed by. Michael Collins delivered the graveside eulogy in Irish and English after the firing of a volley of shots by uniformed Irish Volunteers.

Cathal Brugha: Badly wounded during 1916, which left him permanently lame, he took the anti-Treaty side, refused to surrender during the initial battle of the Civil War and was shot dead on the streets of Dublin on 7 July 1922.

Erskine Childers: He smuggled guns in his yacht the *Asgard* into Ireland in 1914. Convicted on the charge of possessing a pistol during the Civil War, he was executed by firing squad at Beggars Bush Barracks on 24 November 1922. His body was exhumed in 1923 and brought to Glasnevin Cemetery.

Seán MacBride: The only child of well-known Irish revolutionary Maud Gonne and Irish republican Major John MacBride, who was executed for his part in the 1916 Rising. Seán was a founding member of Amnesty International and won the Nobel Peace Prize. Mother and son are buried together. Maud died on 27 April 1953 and Seán on 15 January 1988.

Constance Markievicz: Born Constance Gore-Booth and known as the 'Rebel Countess', she dedicated her life to the cause of Irish freedom and died on 15 July 1927, aged fifty-nine.

Dick McKee: A prominent member of the republican movement. He was killed by the British military in Dublin Castle on Bloody Sunday, 21 November 1920.

Rory O'Connor: He was condemned to death on 8 December 1922 by his once close friend, Minister for Justice Kevin O'Higgins. O'Connor was best man at O'Higgins wedding the year before.

Others lie in family or single plots within the cemetery. These include:

Michael Collins: The nationalist leader from Clonakilty, Co. Cork was killed in the Irish Civil War on 22 August 1922, aged thirty-one. Kathy Barry cried 'buckets' when she heard of his untimely death. His is among the most famous and most visited graves in Glasnevin. Around him were buried at least 183 soldiers of the Irish Free State. In 1967, their names were inscribed on the National Army Memorial surrounding their leader's grave. Fresh flowers continue to adorn his grave to this day.

Éamon de Valera: Republican, nationalist and statesman, who died peacefully at the age of ninety-two on 29 August 1975. His long and varied political career spanned one of the most turbulent periods in Irish history. After a state funeral, he was buried beside his wife and son in the cemetery.

Arthur Griffith: The founder of Sinn Féin, Griffith led the delegation sent to negotiate the Anglo-Irish Treaty that ended the War of Independence. He died aged fifty-one of a cerebral haemorrhage on 12 August 1922.

It is among all these Irish heroes that Kevin Barry now rests.

Of course enemies in life can also share the same ground in death. William Martin Murphy, the instigator of the 1913 Dublin Lockout, who died in June 1919, is buried in a vault in Glasnevin. He was a rich businessman when he died. Murphy's arch-nemesis and Kevin's hero, James Larkin, founder of the Irish Transport and General Workers' Union, died on 30 January 1947 and lies close by.

***

Every year on 1 November, the anniversary of Kevin's death, the Barry family travel from Tombeagh to attend Mass in Clarendon Street,

Dublin. Afterwards, they visit his grave and take a few moments for private meditation. Like W. B. Yeats, Kevin's own words would make a fitting epitaph. In a line from an essay he wrote about having ideals, he stated: 'It brings out all that is good in a man and has given to history many of the noblest of its characters.'

EPILOGUE

IN MEMORY OF

All around us there are things and places to remind us of Kevin Barry and his legacy. In Dublin, the centre at 44 Parnell Square where some of the Volunteers trained is now called Kevin Barry Hall. The junction of Church Street and North King Street, scene of the ill-fated ambush on Monday 20 September 1920, is very different today. A busy thoroughfare, the only clue to past events is the name Kevin Barry on the overlooking local authority flats. There is also a plaque on the wall at 8 Fleet Street, which reads: 'In this house was born Kevin Barry on 20th of January 1902. He died for Ireland on 1st November 1920.'

Kevin's killing deeply affected his fellow students in UCD. They wanted to do something to honour his memory, so they formed the Kevin Barry Memorial Committee shortly after his death. Their main aim was to raise money from students and graduates of the college for a memorial in his honour. Through the sale of a special Kevin Barry memorial card and membership subscriptions, they raised £100 in 1921 and collected another £400 in 1923.

Eventually, in 1933, Richard King of the Harry Clarke studios was commissioned to create a commemorative stained-glass window. It was unveiled in the Earlsfort Terrace campus by committee member Richard O'Rahilly on 1 November 1934. It consists of eight panels, each one depicting a heroic episode of Irish history and the struggle for independence. The figure of Kevin standing to attention in a Fianna uniform dominates most of the lower two right-hand sections. It became one of the college's best-loved features until it was relocated to the Belfield campus in 2011, after being conserved and restored. Now it sits in the Kevin Barry gallery, on the first floor of the Charles Institute of Dermatology building. A special spotlight illuminates the panes in the evening time.

Using modern technology, the Kevin Barry papers are stored as part of the UCD Digital Library and can be easily accessed online. The collection includes material associated with his days at Belvedere College, his year as a medical student in UCD and his brief time in custody in Mountjoy Prison before his execution. The majority of it was collected by his sister Kathy Barry Moloney and was donated by his grandnephew Doctor Eunan O'Halpin in 1990.

The college is also home to the Kevin Barry Cumann. Established in the 1930s, it is one of UCD's oldest societies. In the 1950s it affiliated itself with the Fianna Fáil political party and is the oldest Ógra Fianna Fáil branch in Ireland.

For many years it was the biggest society on campus and was influential in the Student's Union. Many high-profile figures, including actor Chris O'Dowd and presenter Ryan Tubridy, have been involved in the society, as well as several prominent Fianna Fáil politicians over the years. Their annual traditions of a hot whiskey night and trips to the Dáil date back to the founding of the cumann. The members also participate in political activities across the country and act as lobbyists to the Fianna Fáil senior party.

Although his time in the O'Connell School was brief, two of his set squares from the school are now part of the Brother William Allen's private collection in the Military Archives in Cathal Brugha Barracks, Dublin. Also in the collection is a postcard produced by the German-Irish Society in Berlin after the six executions in Mountjoy Prison in March 1921. Depicting six ravens sitting on six hangman's gallows, the caption reads: 'A German view of things, England Hang-Land. Remember Ireland's Gallows.'

Belvedere College currently has a cabinet display with Kevin Barry memorabilia in the foyer. It includes his old school desk, his science notebook, his Belvedere cap, his death warrant, signed by General Macready on 27 October, and the telegram sent to the extended Barry family in Tombeagh at 9.52 a.m. on 1 November, donated by the O'Rahilly family.

Mementos to his legacy are not just to be found in Dublin, however. As a son of Rathvilly, with both sides of his family having lived there for generations, it is not surprising that the Kevin Barry Monument was erected in the centre of the picturesque village. It was unveiled in 1958 by 1916 widow Kathleen Clarke. President de Valera attended the fiftieth anniversary ceremony there in 1970.

Also in 1970, An Post issued a special commemorative stamp to mark the fiftieth anniversary of Kevin's execution. It is a photo of him in his Belvedere rugby jersey that was taken in 1919.

Two books have been written about Kevin Barry. The first, *Kevin Barry*, was written by Seán Cronin and published in 1965. The second, entitled *Kevin Barry and His Time*, was written by Donal O'Donovan and published in 1989. Donal was Kevin's nephew. He completed the research initiated by his father, James, some years before. It contains interviews with family members and rare photographs of the Barry family.

In the National Museum of Ireland, on display in the Soldiers and Chiefs section, there is a copy of the bronze plaque erected in his memory at Monks' Bakery, Church Street. Also on display, 'Our Martyr Boy' is a commemorative pamphlet printed in Buenos Aires in 1921 that includes poems about Kevin Barry. Finally, the museum is home to a small plaster bust of Kevin, approximately eleven inches high, which is kept safely in storage.

Countless Kevin Barry clubs have also sprung up around the world. These are mainly GAA clubs and they stretch from Tyrone to Philadelphia. The Kevin Barry Irish Club in Dutchess County, New York fundraises for Irish people in need in the area.

In 2020, on the centenary of his death, a new generation will learn about Kevin and hopefully some new memorabilia will be produced. We must never forget people like Kevin Barry.

APPENDIX

BALLADS AND POEMS

There are many ballads and poems commemorating the life of Kevin Barry. Here are a few of the best-loved titles.

Recorded and sung by various international artists, including Paul Robeson, Leonard Cohen and Hank Locklin, and Irish artists such as Christy Moore, Damien Dempsey and The Wolfe Tones, the first of these is called 'Kevin Barry'. It was written by an Irish exile in Glasgow around 1920. There are many versions of this song.

'KEVIN BARRY'

1

In Mountjoy Jail one Monday morning
High upon the gallows tree,
Kevin Barry gave his young life
For the cause of liberty.
But a lad of eighteen summers,
Yet no one can deny,
As he walked to death that morning
He proudly held his head on high.

2

'Why not shoot me like a soldier,
Do not hang me like a dog,
For I fought to free old Ireland,
On that bright September morn.
All around that little bakery,
Where we fought them hand to hand.
Why not shoot me like a soldier
For I fought to free Ireland.'

3

Just before he faced the hangman
In his dreary prison cell,
British soldiers tortured Barry
Just because he would not tell
The names of his brave companions,
And other things they wished to know.
'Turn informer or we'll kill you!'
Kevin Barry answered 'No!'

4

Calmly standing to attention,
While he bade his last farewell
To his broken-hearted mother,
Whose sad grief no one can tell,
For the cause he proudly cherished
This sad parting had to be;
Then to death walked, softly smiling,
That old Ireland might be free.

5

Another martyr for old Ireland,
Another murder for the crown,
Whose brutal laws may kill the Irish,
But won't keep their spirit down.
Lads like Barry are no cowards,
From the foe they will not fly;
Lads like Barry will free Ireland,
For her sake they'll live or die.

6

Kevin Barry you must leave us,
On the scaffold you must die,
Cried his broken-hearted mother,
As she bade her son goodbye.
Kevin turned to her in silence,
And said 'Mother do not weep,
For it's all for dear old Ireland,
And it's all for Freedom's sake.'

Another anonymous song is simply called:

'BALLAD'

1

I've a sad but true story to relate
Of a brave young Irishman's cruel fate.
It is written down in the roll of fame
And Kevin Barry is the brave lad's name.

2

When scarcely eighteen years of age
To the Republican Army he was engaged
For Ireland's sake he struck a blow
To free his country from a tyrant foe.

3

In the fight with the foe against the crown
Young Barry shot a British soldier down,
He appeared and was tried by military
And sentenced to die on the gallows tree.

4

In the condemned cell awaiting his fate
He was asked to confess before it was too late:
'Come tell us where your comrades may be
A pardon will be granted and we'll set you free.'

5

Young Barry gazed with a look of scorn:
An Irish traitor yet was never born!
'Carry out your sentence' was the brave reply,
'For Ireland I fought and for Ireland I'll die!'

6

Outside the jail his comrades fell
On their knees in prayer to the prison bell
For to pray for the soul of a martyr friend
Who would rather die than to foemen bend.

7

Out from the jail then walked the priest
And the tears rolled down his manly cheeks;

'Have they hanged him, Father?' his comrades
cried.
'He's gone but a braver lad never died.'

What follows is a selection of poems about Barry. The first was published by Seán Mac Giolla Buidhe in *The Gael* of 6 February 1922:

'CAOIMHGHÍN DE BARRA'

1

Go moch ar maidin 'sa' carchar dubh
Do crochadh de Barra gan taise gan truagh
An t-ógach oilte a throid go tréan
'Uaghaidh foirneart foirtil na mbodach gclaon.

2

Lasmuich bhí mílte ag guidhe go fraoch
Go scaoilfí Caoimhghín as geimheala géar',
Ach b'feárr le Dia é bheith leis féin
Go h-árd 'na ríoghacht í measc na naomh

3

Mar mhairtir déag sé-an buachaill bocht
Gan eagl', réir ba dhual dhá shlíocht,

Ar son a thírín chéabhta thláith
D'fhulaing pianta ghéara chrádha.

4

Ar Láimh Dheis Dé go raibh ár laoch
Le Pádraic Naomhtha is treibh na naomh
Leis an bPiarsach, Aghas, MacSuibhne séim-
Ag guidhne gan spás ar Chlainne Gaedheal

This next one is taken from the *Wolfe Tone Annual* of 1936 and was penned by Countess Markievicz in November 1922.

'KEVIN'

1

We knelt at mass with sobbing hearts
Cold, in the dawn of day.
The dawn for us, for him the night,
Who was so young and gay.

2

Then from the altar spoke the priest,
His voice rang thin with pain –
Bidding us pray, a boy must die
At England's hands again.

3

The cruel English tortured him,
He never shrank or cried;

Sublime his faith, the gallows tree
He faced that day with pride.

4

Proudly he gave his life for her.
To whom his heart was given;
His dying eyes knew freedom near,
Saw death the gate of Heaven.

5

Bright flaming dawn of a young life,
Simple and pure and brave;
One childlike prayerful sacrifice,
His end – a felon's grave.

6

His end! No end to lives like his;
With us he lives always.
Bright through our night, a shining star,
He lights for us the way.

7

And Christ, who died for love of us,
Tortured and bruised and shamed,
Gives courage to such hero souls,
Unbending and untamed.

'THE GALLOWS GRIM'
by Pádraig Widger

1

The gallows grim a group of people kneeling,
The prison grey against a sullen sky,
To our Lady of Sorrows they are pleading
As a youth of tender years walks out to die.

2

See, here he comes with footstep slow and steady,
With upward gaze and lips that move in prayer,
To sacrifice his young life he is ready,
God comfort his poor weeping mother there.

3

Those memories of the past seem left behind us;
What sorrow yet shall be our destiny;
The little wayside crosses still remind us
How brave men died to set their country free.

4

Such were my thoughts as shades of night
surround me,
Living again the past as sad tears flow,
Saying a fervent prayer 'ere morning found me,
For the lad who died for Ireland long ago.

And finally, a poem by Brian O'Higgins, a revolutionary poet and Sinn Féin president from 1931 to 1933, taken from a 1936 calendar. This was chosen because of its very apt last line.

'KEVIN BARRY'

1

They have taken him – a soldier of the people
A boy in years, a man in fearless faith –
They have tried him with a mockery of justice,
And the sentence of his enemy is – death.

2

They have offered him the freedom of the
traitor,
They have hurt him with the cruelty of hell,
But their tortures and their bribes were
unavailing,
No tale of black dishonour would he tell.

3

The hour has come to test a true man's courage,
  No craven fear he feels, no pang of shame,
For God is with him walking to the scaffold,
  And faithful Ireland kneels to bless his name.

4

The deed is done; the tyrant's blow has fallen;
The brave young soldier's hard-fought fight is
  o'er,
The bell is tolled; the prayers are like a chorus –
  And Kevin Barry lives for evermore.

BIBLIOGRAPHY

BOOKS

Carey, Tim, *Hanged For Ireland: 'The Forgotten Ten', Executed 1920–21. A Documentary History* (Blackwater Press, Dublin, 2001)

Cronin, Seán, *The Story of Kevin Barry* (Irish Freedom Press, Dublin, 2001)

Dublin Cemeteries Committee (ed.), *Glasnevin Cemetery: An Historic Walk* (Dublin Cemeteries Committee, Dublin, 1997)

McMahon, Sean, *The War of Independence* (Mercier Press, Cork, 2019)

Meenan, James (ed.), *Centenary History of the Literary and History Society of University College Dublin 1855–1955* (The Kerryman, Tralee, 1955)

O'Donovan, Donal, *Kevin Barry and his Time* (Glendale, Dublin, 1989)

O'Toole, Edward, *Whist for your life, that's treason: Recollections of a Long Life* (Ashfield Press, Dublin, 2003)

Ryan, Philip B., *The Lost Theatres of Dublin* (The Badger Press, Wiltshire, 1989)

ARCHIVES

Military Archive, Ireland
UCD Archive – Kevin Barry Papers

NEWSPAPERS

Daily Mail
Irish Independent
Le Matin
Los Angeles Daily News
The Chicago Tribune

The Freeman's Journal
The Irish Times
The Manchester Guardian
The Morning Post
The New York Tribune
Westminster Gazette

ACKNOWLEDGEMENTS

A big thank you to the Barry family, my colleagues in Dún Laoghaire-Rathdown Library Service and other library services around the country, members of the National Graves Association and Abraxas Writers, the staff of Kevin Barry's schools, University College Dublin, Glasnevin Cemetery, the National Museum of Ireland, the Military Archives and the Irish Copyright Licensing Authority, and everybody at Mercier Press, as well as my many friends and family.